UNDERSTANDING GLOBAL TRADE & COMMERCE

GLOBAL INEQUALITIES & THE FAIR TRADE MOVEMENT

Elisabeth Herschbach

UNDERSTANDING GLOBAL TRADE & COMMERCE

THE ECONOMICS OF GLOBAL TRADE

Kim M. Etingoff

UNDERSTANDING GLOBAL TRADE & COMMERCE

THE GLOBAL ECONOMY & THE ENVIRONMENT

David Peterfalvi

UNDERSTANDING GLOBAL TRADE & COMMERCE

GLOBAL TRADE ORGANIZATIONS

Holly E.

D1365001

The Global Community
Techniques and Strategies of Trade

The Global Community
Techniques and Strategies of Trade

Daniel E. Harmon

MASON CREST
PHILADELPHIA

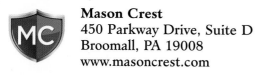

Mason Crest
450 Parkway Drive, Suite D
Broomall, PA 19008
www.masoncrest.com

©2017 by Mason Crest, an imprint of National Highlights, Inc.

Printed and bound in the United States of America.

CPSIA Compliance Information: Batch #CWI2016.
For further information, contact Mason Crest at 1-866-MCP-Book.

First printing
1 3 5 7 9 8 6 4 2

Library of Congress Cataloging-in-Publication Data

on file at the Library of Congress
ISBN: 978-1-4222-3664-2 (hc)
ISBN: 978-1-4222-8119-2 (ebook)

Understanding Global Trade and Commerce series ISBN: 978-1-4222-3662-8

Table of Contents

KEY ICONS TO LOOK FOR:

 Words to Understand: These words with their easy-to-understand definitions will increase the reader's understanding of the text, while building vocabulary skills.

 Sidebars: This boxed material within the main text allows readers to build knowledge, gain insights, explore possibilities, and broaden their perspectives by weaving together additional information to provide realistic and holistic perspectives.

 Research Projects: Readers are pointed toward areas of further inquiry connected to each chapter. Suggestions are provided for projects that encourage deeper research and analysis.

 Text-Dependent Questions: These questions send the reader back to the text for more careful attention to the evidence presented there.

 Series Glossary of Key Terms: This back-of-the book glossary contains terminology used throughout this series. Words found here increase the reader's ability to read and comprehend higher-level books and articles in this field.

Modern container ships are designed to transport hundreds of cargo truck trailers filled with products. That means items do not have to be unloaded from a trailer at the shipping dock, stowed separately aboard the ship, then reloaded onto another truck trailer at the destination port. It results in enormous time and labor savings.

1

Trading Methods Then and Now

The year is 215 BCE. A caravan of traveling traders from the orient has stopped to rest at a *caravanserai* outside Samarkand, a city in central Asia. Here, they find comfortable lodging, food, and drink. Their animals are stabled and fed.

Inside the inn, other traders from near and far engage in conversation with the new arrivals. They are eager to discover what goods are available for trade. Deals are made. Overnight, the contents of the caravan change. By the time it reaches its destination, its cargo will be quite different from what it consisted of when the caravan set forth.

This early trading technique was simple. Goods destined for foreign markets were amassed at trading centers. They were secured aboard donkeys, camels, horses, and other pack animals which were organized into caravans. The caravans set out for distant trading towns and cities. Along the way, they sold some of their goods and acquired additional products.

Caravan travel was extremely dangerous. Thieves lay in wait along the routes. If a traveler suffered a minor medical ailment, only crude treatment was available; the problem quickly could worsen and become life-threatening. Natural elements—droughts, blizzards, floods—killed many traders along the caravan routes.

Scenes similar to the exchange in the caravanserai were common in different ancient cultures on different continents. Traders elsewhere hauled cargoes by rivers, lakes, and coastal waters as well as overland. In most scenarios, the distances were shorter than those traversed by caravans. The basic technique—transporting valuable commodities between trading centers and exchanging goods at stops along the way—was common worldwide.

Massive Cargoes, Faster Voyages

It is January 31, 1858, and the people of London are in a fever of excitement. After almost four years under construction, the *Great Eastern* is about to be launched into the River Thames. Built of iron,

 Words to Understand in This Chapter

caravanserai—an inn with stables where caravans traversing the Middle and Far East could stop to rest and engage in trade with travelers on cross routes.

commodity—an agricultural, mining, or manufacturing product that can be bought and sold in local markets and in international trade.

export—the shipment of products out of a country to buyers in other countries.

magnate—a corporate leader who has become very powerful in a particular area of industry.

trading partner—a person, company, or foreign government with whom regular trade takes place.

The **Great Eastern** *was the largest iron ship ever built to that point in history.*

it is 692 feet (211 meters) long—dwarfing every other ship afloat. Reporters hail it as "The Wonder of the Seas."

Ironically, the *Great Eastern* proved to be a colossal disappointment. It never lived up to its expectations, either as a passenger or cargo carrier. Its thirty-year career was marred by accidents. Many of its backers were driven to financial ruin. Its one great accomplishment was laying the first transatlantic cable—a feat which did contribute greatly to international commerce. The cable expedited communications between Europe and the Americas.

Despite its relative failure, the *Great Eastern* was a sym-

This enormous container ship can barely fit into the Gatun locks of the Panama Canal. Since the canal opened, ships have been designed to the maximum size that can pass through the Canal—a specification known as Panamax.

bol of the times. It represented a new strategy for international commerce: Create larger vessels to deliver more products and passengers in a single voyage. Shipping *magnates* were building larger and faster craft constructed of iron and steel and powered by steam. The second half of the nineteenth century was an era when cargo tonnages and passenger accommodations multiplied. Economically, the nations of the world were being brought together at a phenomenal pace.

The pace would quicken with the construction of canals that shortened shipping routes and altered trade strategies.

In 1869, the Suez Canal was opened across the Isthmus of Suez in Egypt. The 121-mile (165-kilometer) canal linked the Mediterranean Sea with the Red Sea to the south, and the Indian Ocean beyond. Previously, ships traveling between ports in Asia and Europe had to sail around the entire continent of Africa. By using the new canal, ships could save thousands of miles and several weeks. This resulted in tremendous savings in shipping costs.

In 1914, after a decade of construction, the Panama Canal opened, connecting the Pacific and Atlantic oceans. Previously, cargo and passenger vessels traveling between

Work continues on a project to create a third set of locks, which would allow larger ships to transit the Panama Canal. The canal expansion project was finally completed in 2016.

Atlantic and Pacific ports had to pass through the Strait of Magellan, a dangerous route near the southern tip of South America. Now, as with the opening of the Suez Canal, ships could cut weeks of travel time and thousands of miles off their journeys.

Trade Goes Up and Over

It is 1947. A twin-engine, propeller-driven transport plane is crossing the Mediterranean Sea, delivering a supply of prized cotton yarn from Egypt to a textile firm in Great Britain. Below, a merchant ship steams westward, bound for the Strait of Gibraltar and the open Atlantic beyond.

In 1927, Charles Lindbergh made the first airplane crossing of the Atlantic Ocean. By proving it could be done, his epic flight inspired investors to put millions of dollars into international air commerce ventures.

The ship and plane have two things in common. Both are bound for England, and both carry products that are being *exported* by Mediterranean *trading partners*. There are two important differences. Obviously, the ship can carry many times as much cargo as the airplane. However, the plane can make many flights back and forth in the time it takes the ship to make one voyage.

The advent of air transport in the 1920s brought a new dimension to international trade. From then on, buyers could obtain foreign goods very quickly, if they needed or wanted them badly enough and were able to afford the

 Watchdog of World Trade

The agency responsible for enforcing international trade laws and agreements today is the World Trade Organization. It hears disputes between trading partners and monitors trading practices around the world.

Created in 1994 and headquartered in Geneva, Switzerland, the WTO assumed wider powers than previous governing bodies. Its predecessor was GATT, representatives of countries that had signed the General Agreement on Tariffs and Trade. GATT had overseen only the exchange of merchandise among countries. The World Trade Organization additionally has authority over international services (Internet, telephone, etc.) and protects the rights of intellectual property owners.

Representatives of member governments negotiate and make the rules by which the WTO acts. Besides regulating import and export activities, the organization's objective is to assist product sellers and service providers in promoting and transacting their businesses across borders. It provides technical training and aid for developing countries.

As of November 2015, 162 nations were WTO members. The administration consists of more than 600 staff workers under the supervision of a director-general.

Cargo is loaded onto an aircraft.

much higher cost of air service. In the jet age today, products can be delivered overnight from a seller in one continent to a buyer in another.

Fast-Forward: Keyboard Transactions

The time is today. An elementary school teacher wants to use hand puppets to illustrate the role various plant and animal species play in the environmental food chain. A quick Internet search locates a promising set of puppet characters: a bear, a fox, a fish, a honeybee, a talking oak tree trunk.

Today, products from all over the world are available online, and can be purchased almost instantly using computers, tablets, phones, and many other devices.

Workers in a distribution center prepare goods that will be shipped to fill online orders.

Several online sellers offer the puppet series. The teacher selects the best bargain and submits a purchase order to the school administration.

The puppets are made in the Philippines. They are in stock and available immediately at a retail distribution center in Kentucky. The order is placed electronically. Two days later, the teacher's new project props arrive at the school.

International Commerce

Changing techniques of global trade—the methods of producing and delivering goods—have led to changing trade strategies among nations. A country's ability to produce a *commodity* cheaply and export it to foreign markets at a profit is critical. International trading strategies largely are based on the production and transportation techniques that are available and most economical.

As shown above, the techniques and strategies employed by traders in the global marketplace have changed greatly during the course of history. They continue to change.

 # Text-Dependent Questions

1. What was the nationality of the *Great Eastern*?
2. What was the agency overseeing international trade that preceded the World Trade Organization?

 # Research Project

Determine, approximately, the distance and time savings that shipping companies began to realize by using the Panama and Suez canals. Using geographical statistics from Internet research, calculate the number of miles (kilometers) along the eastern and western coasts of South America and Africa. Present to the class simple maps of South America and Africa, helping impress the distances in miles (kilometers) that ships saved by using the canals. Also find estimates of the days and weeks voyages take when using the canals, compared to the time it takes to round the continental capes.

Today, many countries have a free market economy, in which private citizens—rather than the government—own and run companies. Businesses compete with each other to sell goods and services. Citizens decide how they want to spend their money in order to provide for their basic needs; excess funds can be used to satisfy their wants.

2

The World of Deal-Makers

The earliest humans learned that they could improve their living conditions by trading with neighbors. They traded foodstuffs, furs for clothing, and primitive weapons and tools.

At first, trade occurred only between near neighbors. It was dangerous to carry trading goods across long distances. Unexpected forces of natures and unfriendly peoples might intervene. Long-distance trading also diverted hunter-gatherer peoples from their daily tasks of survival.

Gradually, trading distances lengthened. Regular trade routes were established through woodlands and deserts, and by boat along waterways. In time, commerce was initiated among traders of far-flung cultures and locations. Trade between civilizations in Europe and Asia began more than 2,000 years ago. Much of it occurred along the fabled Silk Road, a network of trade routes that linked China, India, and the Roman Empire.

As they traveled across oceans and continents, traders contributed to the knowledge of *geographers* and historians. They recorded information about places, distances, natural features of the earth's surface, and cultures.

The quest for trade opportunities and wealth was the primary incentive that drove the age of European exploration which began in the fifteenth century. It began in earnest under the guidance of Prince Henry of Portugal (1394–1460), who came to be known as "Henry the Navigator." Henry was intrigued by the study of navigation and the limitless possibilities of ocean commerce. He found-

 # Words to Understand in This Chapter

assembly line—a factory arrangement where a product being manufactured passes along a line; at each process point, a worker or machine performs one assembly task.

colony—a territory claimed and governed by a powerful nation far away.

geographer—a scientist who studies the natural and cultural features of different places around the world.

mass production—the assembly of many copies of the same product at the same time, using a system that combines machines and human workers for assembly.

perishables—goods that must be distributed and delivered quickly because they will spoil in a matter of days or weeks.

spinning jenny—a machine with multiple spindles (protruding sticks) used to spin cotton and wool into thread.

staple—a major commodity or manufactured item produced for trade in a country, region, or city.

wages—earnings paid to a laborer.

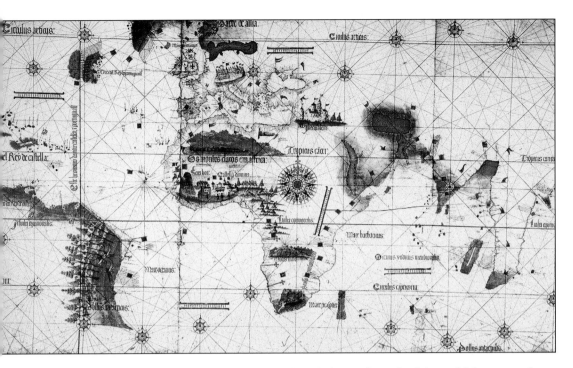

This Portuguese map from 1501 shows the detailed coastline of Africa, which Portugal had been exploring for many years, as well as vague information about newly discovered lands to the west (Brazil) and east (India). Small colorful flags denote the locations of trading posts operated by various European nations.

ed a school for navigators. He sent forth Portuguese expeditions to bring back information about the west African coast and its trading ports.

By the 1600s, ships from Spain, Portugal, the Netherlands, France, and Great Britain were engaged in trading expeditions that reached thousands of miles from their home ports. Explorers—often backed by well-armed ships—negotiated trading agreements with kingdoms in India, Africa, and Asia, and across the Atlantic in the Americas.

European merchants formed trading companies that became very powerful factors in international politics. In many remote ports, it was the trading companies, not military forces, that initially established European control and represented the interests of their home countries. Notable among them were the Dutch East India Company, which controlled the lucrative spice trade of the Indonesian islands; the British East India Company, which gained control over large areas of India; and the Hudson's Bay Company, which established the British *colony* in Canada during the seventeenth century.

 ## Merchants Find Strength in Unity

During the late Middle Ages (approximately 1100–1300), European kingdoms and cities began to forge treaties setting forth the legal rights of visiting traders. They organized trade associations. Most notable was the Hanseatic League, which at one time had merchant members in more than 100 German cities and towns.

The strategy of forming trade alliances provided several benefits to member merchants. The associations negotiated with government authorities to obtain trading privileges for their members. They funded military actions against pirates and highway bandits. Traveling together afforded league members a degree of protection from robbers and savage beasts.

Merchants of the Hanseatic League packed goods over long distances, from the North Sea and Baltic Sea to trading centers around the Mediterranean. Trade goods included raw materials such as furs and timber; foodstuffs including salt and salted fish, fruits, grains, oils, honey, wine, and spices; cloth and garments; and jewels. Merchants used pack animals on overland trails. Other traders traveled by water. They used longboats and small ships along the coasts of the Baltic and North seas, smaller vessels on rivers and canals.

Railroads were created during the nineteenth century, and soon became the dominant method of transporting people and goods. Although other forms of transportation, including cars and airplanes, have replaced the train for most passenger travel, the railroad is still one of the most cost-efficient ways to transport goods across large land areas, such as the western United States and Canada.

Trade-driven exploration was not the exclusive province of Europeans. The Polynesians of the South Pacific, for example, were noted for their durable canoe construction and their knowledge and instincts for navigation. They traded goods from island to island hundreds of miles apart using these small but seaworthy craft.

Changing Trade Strategies

Global trade strategies and techniques began changing rap-

Development of oil sands in Alberta, Canada. The sands include thick petroleum deposits that, thanks to modern technology, can be processed into crude oil. Petroleum is a major industry in Canada, and the country ranks fifth in the world in oil production.

idly in the mid-1800s. Many of the changes were brought about by the Industrial Revolution. Others were caused by shifts in agriculture and the workforce. Once-dominant crops waned in importance; new ones took their place. Organized labor in industrialized nations impacted *wages* and the profitability of manufacturing certain products.

Changes in transportation also affected trade. Wagon roads were improved. Railroads expanded throughout North America and Europe and began to reach across other continents. Tons of products could be move between industrial centers faster and cheaper by rail than in the old days of wagon transport.

And new trade goods became popular as European explorers spread into frontier regions that held resources previously unknown to them. For instance, beginning in the 1800s, the mining of raw minerals increased in certain regions of Canada. This led to the establishment and expansion of manufacturing. Manufactured products became one of Canada's most important international exports. They still are today.

Governments and companies had to adapt to the changes. Global trade never would be the same as in past generations. Change—much of it unpredictable—became a constant factor in coming up with international trade strategies.

The Industrial Revolution

In a nutshell, the Industrial Revolution was a dramatic shift from producing goods by hand to producing them with machines. It was the golden age of inventions. *Spinning jennies*, steam engines, improved techniques of metalworking, and many other innovations made it possible to produce *staple* commodities much faster and with less human labor than before.

The Industrial Revolution began in Great Britain in the late 1700s. Inventors were intent on improving the way machines worked. Business leaders began realizing the benefits of *mass production*. Factories began making more products in less time than it took before.

Since the 1860s, when an inexpensive process for manufacturing steel in large quantities was developed, steel has been one of the most important elements of the world's industrial economy.

The "revolution" quickly spread to America. Factories devised **assembly lines** where each worker was assigned to perform just one task as a product was moved along. In this way, astonishing quantities of sophisticated products could be produced in a short time. For example, the Ford Motor Company built some 15 million Model T automobiles in less than 20 years, beginning in 1908.

One result of the Industrial Revolution was that thousands of people who previously farmed for a living began migrating to cities. There, they could find steady work, even though the wages were meager and the work was often exhausting and dangerous. By contrast, farm harvests were unpredictable from year to year. Unfavorable seasonal weather and crop diseases could ruin a farmer in a single year.

The Industrial Revolution occurred in western countries that were technically developed. But it greatly affected trade worldwide. To an extent, the transition from old to new production techniques still is occurring in third world countries. It fundamentally has changed the way people

Laborers and robots work together on the assembly line of a Ford Motors factory in Yelabuga, Russia. The assembly line was one of many innovations that made manufacturing more efficient.

live—the way they work, the kinds of products they consume, how products are made and distributed, product prices, and the cost of making those products.

The Rise of Labor Unions

The Industrial Revolution enabled manufacturers to produce more and more trade goods with machines rather than by hand. However, this did not relieve workplace stress on laborers. In some ways, the operation of machines presented new hazards. Employers pressed their employees to put in long work days to produce more goods.

In the United States, 11.1 percent of wage earners and salaried workers were members of unions in 2015, according to the U.S. Bureau of Labor Statistics. They numbered 14.8 million workers. Union membership in the U.S. has been declining in recent decades. In 1983, 17.7 million workers (20.1 percent of the U.S. workforce) belonged to unions.

Countries Unite for Trading Purposes

Just as workers found bargaining power by forming labor unions, so did nations. Countries with common economic interests have joined to form trading blocs around the globe. A primary example, which became a model for later economic unions, is Benelux.

The Benelux Economic Union is a trading agreement involving Belgium, the Netherlands, and Luxembourg—three neighboring countries. The three nations signed the agreement in 1960, but the beginnings of Benelux can be traced to some years earlier. A number of international organizations were forged after World War II (1939–1945) to promote cooperation in trade.

The Benelux countries impose the same tariff rates for imports that arrive from other countries. For trade among themselves, no tariffs are charged.

Benelux became an important example of how countries could unite and promote economic benefits for all member nations. In fact, Benelux is considered a model which led to the formation of the European Union in 1993.

European workers in the late 1700s began to band together to demand higher wages and reduced hours. In some industrialized countries, governments at first passed laws banning unions. They feared the workers' demands would hamper trade. However, social reformers during the nineteenth century gradually achieved better working conditions. The use of small children to perform manual work, for example, was abandoned. Labor unions became established and accepted.

Advances in Transportation

The camel caravans and rickety cargo ships and boats of yesteryear became almost extinct by the early twentieth century. Iron ships and barges powered by coal and steam took over commerce on oceans, rivers, and lakes. On land, rail lines spread across the continents. The trucking industry was born. With road expansion and improvement, products could be hurried across miles of countryside, from warehouse to warehouse. Both sea and land transportation advances led to increased international commerce.

Then came the airplane. Entrepreneurs foresaw the potential for profit in transporting merchandise and passengers.

Airmail service began in North America in 1918. At first, it was used only to expedite urgent mail between major cities. By 1921, important mail was being delivered from coast to coast. As the airline industry grew and service became more reliable, airmail began to spread worldwide. Soon, improved aerial navigation and lighted runways enabled night flights.

Governments and private companies realized airplanes could be used to transport much more than mail. Within a few years, air commerce was flourishing. It developed quickly in Europe. Government airlines used planes to transport passengers and goods between the home countries and their colonies.

Ship, rail, and truck transport did not cease after air commerce began. Even today, they continue to be vital in linking world economies. For fast shipments, though—especially important for emergency items and *perishable* commodities—air delivery is preferred, even though it generally costs more.

 Text-Dependent Questions

1. Over a period of two decades beginning in 1908, how many Model T cars did the Ford Motor Company produce?
2. In what year did airmail service begin in North America?

 Research Project

Using the Internet or your school library, find out about the European "scramble for Africa" in the late 1800s. Create a map of Africa as it was divided into European colonies as of 1900. Explain to the class why certain countries wanted to control certain regions of Africa.

Textile workers in a small factory in Delhi, India. Today, more than 60 percent of world clothing exports are manufactured in developing countries. Asia is the major world supplier, producing more than 32 percent of the world's clothing exports.

3

Operating in the Global Economy

By the mid-twentieth century, international trading strategies and tactics had become very different from what they were less than a century earlier. As we have seen, dramatic changes were brought about by astonishing advances in production and transportation.

Change continues today at an even faster pace. Technological advances have brought people around the world close together in significant ways. We instantly can communicate with individuals half a world away. We can order a product from a distant continent and expect delivery in days, whereas a century ago it would have taken months. The ways in which products are marketed and distribution is managed are very different now.

All the while, foreign policies have become more complicated. Relationships among peoples and governments are affected deeply by the changing nature of global trade and commerce.

Economic issues are central in shaping friendships—and competition—among nations of all continents.

Taxes and Customs

Countries have levied *customs* duties on cross-border trade since ancient times. Governments receive *revenue* by imposing taxes on products that traders export and import. In this way, they not only bring in more money for the government; they also influence the prices of products that are exchanged among countries. They help protect the trade value of goods produced in their own countries.

For example, North Americans buy countless products

 Words to Understand in This Chapter

brand—in business, an immediately identifiable feature that lets everyone know who the company is.

customs—taxes charged by a government on products entering or leaving a country.

incentive—a benefit, such as low taxes, offered to a trading organization by the home government or a foreign government.

lobby—to try to persuade legislators and public officials to pass laws and take actions that will be favorable to the lobbying corporation or organization.

logo—a distinctive emblem that identifies a company in consumers' minds.

offshoring—having work or services performed by employees overseas.

revenue—the money a government takes in by taxing its own citizens and by taxing import and export goods.

slogan—an attention-getting phrase ingrained in consumers' minds for marketing purposes.

Trade and financial agreements are at the heart of many foreign policy strategies and techniques. Military powers, for example, come to terms with one another based in large part on what economic benefits each will receive from the agreement.

that are made inexpensively overseas, thanks to cheap labor in those countries. An import tax can raise the price of those items significantly. Thus, American consumers ultimately may find that it is just as cheap, or almost as cheap, to buy certain of those items from American manufacturers.

Custom taxes are money a government demands from companies moving products into or out of the country. A custom tax also is known as a duty.

Countries negotiate various treaties among themselves that pertain to commerce. For instance, some tax treaties

There were more than 36,000 McDonald's fast food restaurants around the world as of 2016, including this one in Moscow, Russia. The company says it serves customers in more than 100 countries on six continents, employing almost 2 million workers.

eliminate or reduce double taxation on visiting workers. This permits people to work in foreign countries and not have to pay earnings taxes both in their home country and in the country of employment.

Business companies are not entirely helpless in controlling their international operations. Large corporations *lobby* their governments to adopt and enforce strategies and policies that will benefit them. They also negotiate with leaders of foreign countries where they do business.

International Companies

Businesses that operate in two or more nations are called multinational corporations, or MNCs. In past centuries, an MNC was headquartered in its home country and opened foreign stores or offices in order to sell its products in those distant locales. Now, many MNCs not only sell their goods in foreign countries but also produce them there.

Offshoring has become a widely adopted business strategy since the early 1990s. Specific techniques are known as production offshoring and offshore outsourcing. In production offshoring, a company based in one country establishes factories in other countries, hiring native workers to assemble its goods. Outsourcing mainly refers to hiring

 ## Employing Technology to Expedite Production and Shipments

Robots have been used for years on factory assembly lines. Much of the assembly of automobiles and thousands of other consumer products is done not by human hands, but by intricately programmed machines.

The shipment and delivery of trade goods internationally also has been improved by technology. Not many generations ago, a sail-powered cargo ship required dozens of sailors to work it from port to port, continent to continent. Voyages took weeks and months. Violent storms caused delays, deaths, and sinkings. Now, a small crew can take a gigantic container ship or oil tanker on a voyage of thousands of miles in a relatively short time. Because of the vessel's size and sophisticated navigational equipment, they have little to fear from stormy weather.

Meanwhile, technology has changed the way product packaging and distribution is managed. Amazon and other retail order fulfillment centers have begun using robots to help process thousands of product orders that are placed online by customers.

technically trained personnel in foreign countries to perform services such as computer support.

Companies do not set up operations abroad merely to build their reputations. Profit is the only meaningful reason to expand overseas. In order to earn the highest profits, they lobby and negotiate with foreign governments to win trade *incentives*.

When deciding where to expand, they look for locations where they can function at a low cost. They choose places that are rich in the natural resources needed to produce their wares. They look for inexpensive local labor—workers who demand lower wages than workers in other countries. They require laborers who are skilled in the necessary manufacturing or service tasks, or who can be trained quickly. They also expect rewards from foreign governments such as low business taxes. In some countries, governments are willing to offer tax and other business credits in order to bring in foreign employers. This creates new jobs for their native work forces.

Marketing—Establishing a Worldwide Brand

Livestock branding has been a trading technique for approximately 4,000 years, historians believe. Using a hot iron, ranchers scar the flanks of their cattle and horses with a shape that everyone recognizes as the *brand* of the owner. In years past, when livestock grazed freely on the open prairies, the brand was proof that an animal belonged to a particular rancher. Today, it serves a more significant

The entrance to a Disney store in Tokyo, Japan. The Walt Disney Corporation is a multi-national producer of entertainment, and Disney is one of the world's most valuable brands.

purpose: It is a mark of quality, the owner's symbol of pride.

Successful multinational companies have established worldwide brands. Some of the most famous brands are the golden arches of McDonald's, the red and white Coca-Cola *logo*, Apple Computer's bitten apple silhouette, and the distinctive block shape of Jeep models. Those products are sold around the world. In every country, consumers instantly recognize the brands.

Chinese workers assemble electronic devices in a factory in Shenzhen. Since the late 1970s the Chinese government has allowed foreign companies to invest in manufacturing facilities in Shenzhen. This helped make Shenzhen and other areas that the government designated "special economic zones" into manufacturing centers.

Branding can be accomplished in other ways besides visual emblems. Catchy broadcast commercial jingles bring to mind major products and services. Companies and organizations copyright and constantly advertise easy-to-remember *slogans* that summarize in a few words what they are noted for.

Over time, brands begin to convey the reputations of certain products. For example, many consumers immediately think of "Starbucks" at the mention of "coffee." The term "Rolls-Royce" translates subconsciously as "luxury car."

 ## Text-Dependent Questions

1. Who benefits from a customs tax—the seller, the buyer, or a government?
2. What is so distinctive about the Jeep brand of automobile?

 ## Research Project

Investigate the advantages of using robots for various facets of commerce, especially product assembly and distribution processing. What are some of the well-recognized companies that use robotics?

The Internet came into existence in the late 1970s. As of the early 1980s, only a few hundred computers were connected to it. Today, Internet users around the world number in the billions.

4

The Internet Alters Everything

Until this century, practically all commerce was conducted in person. In ages past, merchandise was sold in tents and *bazaars* and in the open air. In later centuries, most merchants have been housed in brick-and-mortar (or wooden) stores and shops. Until quite recently, a significant percentage of wares were peddled door to door by traveling salespeople.

Consumers still enjoy shopping in person. Products such as fresh foods continue to be more conveniently available at local marketplaces. Increasingly, though, shoppers in different countries are making most of their purchases online. Why? Because the Internet makes it easy and presents shopping options that consumers never had before. They can find practically anything they want or need on the Internet. They even can order packaged and canned foods online, often finding better prices than in their neighborhood supermarkets.

Advantages of Electronic Commerce

Convenience is the most obvious advantage of shopping online. A product can be ordered and paid for by credit or debit card in a minute or two, using a mobile phone or tablet computer. The purchase can be transacted wherever the buyer happens to be at the moment: at home, at work, on campus, in a park, or in a car or bus.

Electronic commerce also fulfills the desire for instant gratification. When modern shoppers decide they want something, they want to have it quickly—immediately, if possible. Most products ordered online can be delivered in two or three days. For a little extra, they can be sent overnight. Only a few categories of shipments take longer to deliver. They mainly are products that have been adver-

 Words to Understand in This Chapter

back-order—when a merchant takes a customer's order for a product that has been sold out; the merchant has to order more of the product from the manufacturer or a distributor, and the customer must wait until a new supply comes in.

bazaar—in ancient Persia and other Middle Eastern cultures, a market consisting of rows of stalls from which merchants sold various goods; the equivalent in the Internet age is the diversity of online sellers.

collectible—an unusual item of trade that may be of no interest to typical consumers but may be very valuable in the minds of collectors; examples are antiques, old coins and stamps, and vintage art.

pharmaceutical—a drug prescribed by doctors and sold to their patients at pharmacies or via online sellers.

stock-based—a company that sells shares of its value to investors.

Orders placed online are typically delivered within a few days. Amazon.com, an online company, has become the largest retailer in the world. It originated in the 1990s as a bookseller, but has since expanded to carry an enormous variety of products.

tised but not yet produced, and products that the online vendor has sold out and has to **back-order**. They also include products that are shipped directly from the foreign countries in which they were made.

Another advantage of e-commerce is the ability for consumers to comparison shop. They do not have to spend hours driving from store to store seeking the best prices. In minutes, without leaving home, they can compare prices offered by online vendors. Web browsing also enables them to quickly find and order rare items, some of which previously were practically unavailable.

Online purchasing frequently, though not always, saves costs over in-store shopping. Store owners have to budget for overhead: the costs of purchasing or leasing the building, heating, air-conditioning, water services, cleaning and maintenance, merchandise displays. A large online warehouse operation has many of the same expenses, but it can function at less cost per square foot because one building houses much more merchandise.

In the long run, transportation cost savings also add up. Consumers don't have to leave their homes on shopping excursions. Suppliers don't have to transport commodities from warehouses to retail outlets; they can ship products directly from a warehouse to consumers.

Online Bazaars and Auctions

Well-known examples of online trading companies are Amazon.com and eBay. They started in the 1990s as little more than visions in the minds of their founders. Today, they are leading players in the worldwide marketing and sales of hundreds of categories of products.

Amazon began by selling books. It soon expanded into selling practically everything. The online book catalog was introduced in 1995 with little publicity. Within a few months, it was selling thousands of books all over the world. It became a *stock-based*, public company in 1997. The next year, it began selling movies and music recordings. A year later, it added thousands of new products: computer software, tools, gift items, pet supplies, *pharmaceuticals*, foods, recreational products, and much more. It

According to figures reported in March 2016 by the DMR statistical news source, the eBay online auction site had some 162 million users shopping for products offered by approximately 25 million sellers. An estimated $82 billion in merchandise was sold via eBay in 2015.

launched an online auction service, selling a variety of *collectibles*.

eBay was launched at about the same time as Amazon. Today, it has operations in some 30 countries. It oversees billions of dollars in international sales annually. Shoppers who locate an item of interest on eBay can place a bid and continue bidding against other bidders until the auction expires. In many instances, they can "buy it now" for a price specified by the seller and receive it quicker (the "instant gratification" instinct). There is no charge for buy-

The development of online banking enabled people to deposit funds, transfer money, and pay bills from the comfort of their home.

ers to bid and transact purchases on eBay. Sellers must pay eBay to have their products listed, and eBay receives a small share of sales profits.

Online Banking

A few consumers began to do some of their banking routines online as early as the late 1980s. Over the next two decades, consumers were leery but increasingly interested in managing their money online. Today, transacting financial activities online from mobile devices is common in many countries. Bank customers can make deposits and withdrawals in a few minutes or even just a few seconds from their laptop PCs, mobile phones, or tablet computers. Many young consumers cannot imagine how they or anyone else could have handled their financial affairs offline.

Online, consumers can manage their money without having to go to the bank. In a minute or two, they can make transactions not just within their home countries but abroad. This new banking convenience is a boon for many, but it raises suspicions among watchdogs of Internet commerce.

 ## Text-Dependent Questions

1. How long does it typically take to order a product online, using a computer or mobile device with a credit or debit card in hand? Less than 2 seconds or less than 2 minutes?
2. What does the term "instant gratification" mean in consumer shopping?

 ## Research Project

Explore the history of the Internet by logging onto the Internet itself. Find details about early networks including ARPANET. Learn how the Internet came into use as a technique of international commerce. Present your findings in class.

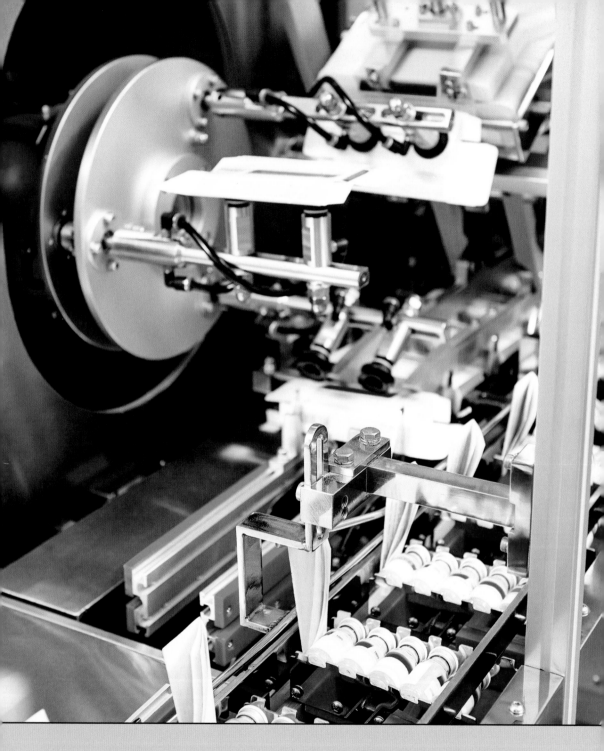

Patents enable pharmaceutical companies to profit from selling the drugs they have spent years developing and testing. Without this protection, anyone could duplicate a drug and there would be no incentive for companies to engage in expensive research and development of new medications.

5

Sticky Issues

Problems and tensions in global trade and commerce are inevitable. One issue that has concerned manufacturers, consumers, and the governments of various countries is related to the protection of intellectual property. The advent of a "world community" connected by the Internet has made intellectual property more vulnerable than ever to theft.

Intellectual property is a work of creativity—a product of the mind. Creative artists—writers, musicians, visual artists, architects, even software engineers—are considered to have the right to profit from their work or inventions.

Intellectual property is different from a product built by hand or on a factory assembly line. Like manufactured goods, intellectual property is a sellable product that has monetary value. But intellectual property often has value to the greater society, so laws have been passed to protect the rights of whose who create it. Societies want to reward the people who create and contribute to the society by making it hard for other people to steal their ideas. Without this protection, there would be no incentive for people to make new inventions or write new books that inspire others.

There are three main types of intellectual property. Each category is designed to legally protect a mental creation.

Copyrights

Some types of intellectual property are fairly easy to understand. A novel, for example, is intellectual property. A talented author wrote the book and therefore deserves to reap profits, if the book sells, in the form of *royalties*.

A hit song is intellectual property. So are the millions of other songs that never make the *Billboard* charts, receive airplay, or sell a single copy. The song lyrics are the proper-

 Words to Understand in This Chapter

pirating—the unauthorized copying and sale or free distribution of creative works for which the copyright owner is entitled to be paid.

royalties—percentages of sales of creative works owed to the authors or composers.

utilities—computer applications used to perform basic tasks such as e-mail handling, malware protection, and managing calendars and schedules.

Bestselling author Jim Ottaviani signs a copy of his graphic novel for a fan. Copyright law protects the works of writers like Ottaviani, preventing people from making and selling copies of their work without permission.

ty of the person who wrote the words. The melody and arrangement are the property of the person who composed the music. In some cases, the writer and composer are the same creative individual. In other cases, two, three, a half dozen or more creative people become involved in "ownership" of the song as it goes through alterations before finally being published and/or recorded.

A painting, drawing, or sculpture is a creative work.

The artist has a right to earn money from his or her work, and can prevent others from copying the work for profit.

In the electronics industry, computer software—such as office programs, games, *utilities*, apps—is intellectual property. If the programmer holds the rights to the work, he or she is entitled to receive royalties from each sale of the program.

Literary, musical, visual, and other creative works can be copyrighted. The creator (or an authorized agent, such as a lawyer or publisher) submits an original copy or facsimile of the work to the government agency that oversees

Some of the world's best-known brands include Google, McDonald's, Nike, Coca-Cola, Facebook, Apple, and others pictured here.

copyrights. Once issued, the copyright proves that the creator owned the work as of the copyright registration date. Any later claim of ownership made by someone who tries to copy the work obviously will be proved bogus.

Copyright does not last forever. In the United States and the European Union, the copyright protection on a book, song, computer program, or other intellectual property typically lasts for the creator's lifetime plus an additional seventy years. In Canada, copyright protection lasts for the creator's lifetime plus fifty years.

Works on which the copyright protection has expired—such as the plays of Shakespeare or the music of Mozart—are said to be in the public domain. This means that anyone can reproduce these works as they see fit. Once something is in the public domain, it is considered to be the property of everyone in society.

Trademarks

A trademark is much simpler to express than a copyrighted work—but it is no less difficult to protect in the world of trade. A trademark is a word, short phrase, or visual symbol (a logo) that distinctively identifies a manufacturer or service provider's product. Many companies and organizations apply to the government to trademark the company name and/or its main products. Coca-Cola is a trademarked soft drink, for instance. Starbucks is a trademarked brand of coffee products. Kodak and Polaroid are long-recognized trademarks in the camera market.

Products such as those sold by Coca-Cola and

McDonald's are recognized by governments around the world as trademarked goods. No other soft-drink company can produce a drink and call it Coca-Cola, or sell a hamburger called a Big Mac. Corporations expect their trademarked commodities to be legally protected from imitation or other misuse in any country.

Patents

A patent is intended to protect an invention. The inventor submits a patent application to the appropriate government agency. The application is accompanied by a detailed description of the invention, how it is assembled, and what it is designed to do. The applicant also submits drawings of the invention.

A patent examiner carefully reviews the application to verify that the invention is unique. During the course of the review, the official may examine the applicant, asking questions about the invention. The review process can take many months before a patent is awarded or denied.

Patents apply to a wide range of products. They include mechanical inventions (entire machines as well as separate working parts), electrical and electronic inventions, packaging designs, chemical compounds such as pharmaceutical drugs, tire and shoe tread patterns, and much more. The term of protection provided by a US patent is either fifteen or twenty years, depending on the type of product patented. In Canada and the European Union, the protective term is twenty years after the patent was filed with the government.

CDs and DVDs for sale at a store in the Guangdong province of China. It is likely that many of these are pirated versions that do not result in royalty payments to the original creator or rights holder.

International IP Issues

National governments have established agencies to deal with intellectual property claims. In the United States, the government agency that oversees copyright registration is the U.S. Copyright Office. Overseeing patents and trademarks is the U.S. Patent and Trademark Office. In Canada, the Canadian Intellectual Property Office handles copyright, patent, and trademark filings.

Protecting Intellectual Property

By the mid-1800s, the ownership of creative works in foreign countries was a serious concern of noted writers and composers. They realized they were losing royalties that they could be earning overseas.

The most important measure for securing their international rights was the Berne Convention. French author Victor Hugo pressed government leaders for a gathering of international government representatives to uphold the French literary concept known as "right of the author." The meeting was held in Berne, Switzerland, in 1886. The agreement that emerged became known as the Berne convention.

Basically, the agreement requires that all nations that signed the pact honor a copyright that is owned by a creator from any country. Before then, most nations' copyright protection applied only inside the country that issued the copyright. That meant a work could be copied overseas, without the copyright holder's knowledge or permission, and sold.

Where problems with international property become very sticky is where physical inventions and creative works enter the world marketplace. There, fully protecting the rights of IP owners is challenging. A patent issued to an inventor in the United States, for example, offers no protection in foreign countries. The inventor must apply for a patent in each country where the product is expected to be sold.

Worldwide copyright enforcement has been made easier by international agreements. Most nations, including the United States and Canada, are members of the Berne Convention, which was originally created in 1886 and has been revised numerous times. Member nations agree to uphold copyright protection for works that were created by authors, composers, and artists in other countries.

A more recent treaty for protecting intellectual property throughout the world is the Agreement on Trade-Related Aspects of Intellectual Property Rights (TRIPS) of 1994. All 162 member nations of the World Trade Organization were required to sign the TRIPS agreement.

In 1996, 188 nations that are part of a United Nations agency called the World Intellectual Property Organization (WIPO) signed a new international treaty that expanded copyright protection to computer programs and information in databases. The WIPO Copyright Treaty also ensured additional copyright protections to authors and creators that were not covered under the Berne Convention. To date, 96 nations have ratified the treaty.

Unfortunately, the Internet and the widespread use of digital media have made global copyright protection and enforcement much more difficult. The ability of unscrupulous people to distribute and/or sell *pirated* products online and on disc media has frustrated intellectual property owners. Pirating costs American musicians, artists, and writers billions of dollars every year in unpaid royalties. The loss is felt especially by the music industry. Digital recordings of copyrighted songs are shared worldwide across the Internet. So are unauthorized copies of lyric sheets, chord sheets, and musical notation.

Creators and publishers of copyrighted works have tried to prevent unauthorized distribution of their works online. Pirating continues to be rampant, however. A 2012 study

Under the terms of the international Agreement on Trade-Related Aspects of Intellectual Property Rights (TRIPS), computer software is considered a "literary work."

by the Business Software Alliance found that China had the highest piracy rate with regards to software, with 77 percent of computer users running pirated software on their PCs. This amounted to more than $9 billion, while legitimate software sales in China were less than $3 billion. Russia and India were next on the list, with 63 percent using pirated software. The United States, the world's largest software market, reported the lowest piracy rate at just 19 percent—however, that still meant there was nearly $10 billion in pirated software being used by American consumers. Although the World Trade Organization and other groups have tried to halt piracy, to date their efforts have been ineffective.

 Text-Dependent Questions

1. What is the difference between copyright, trademark, and patent protection?
2. What international agreement, originally signed in 1886, helps copyright holders secure their rights abroad?

 Research Project

Research the history of famous products such as Coca-Cola, Kodak, and Polaroid. What is their stature in the world marketplace today?

Protesters in Toronto march against the proposed Trans-Pacific Partnership, a free-trade agreement signed by twelve Pacific Rim countries in February 2016. Free trade has been stimulating national economies, but criticized for eliminating jobs and disrupting communities in the United States, Canada, and elsewhere.

Global Commerce in the 21st Century

The exact nature of international trade in coming years is a question mark. Economic trends and conditions constantly are shifting. *Economists* and business advisors constantly study developments and publish forecasts. However, it is impossible to predict what global markets will be like in 2020, 2030, 2050, or the next millennium.

Supply and demand for products frequently change in world markets. Methods of commercial communication and transportation steadily advance. International trade techniques and strategies always will vary to conform with current trends and improvements.

Political as well as economic analysts keep a close eye on developments in international commerce. The exchange of goods among nations affects countries' overall relations and policies. Certain commercial subjects will be of particular interest to observers in coming years.

The European Union (EU)

Economists and political observers are intently monitoring activities and developments of the European Union (EU). The league was formed after decades of negotiations among European leaders. Their basic strategy is simple: to achieve political strength and economic benefits in unity. Many watchers believe the EU collectively is becoming a world "superpower" not unlike the United States and Russia.

Twenty-eight countries now comprise the European Union. It formally was established by a treaty in 1993. The euro became the standard monetary unit in most member nations beginning in 2002. A number of governing institutions have been established. They include the European Parliament, Court of Justice of the European Union, and

 Words to Understand in This Chapter

economist—a specialist in the study of how goods and services are produced, marketed, distributed, and consumed.

entrepreneur—a person who launches a new, perhaps risky business enterprise.

nuclear energy—power created by splitting or fusing atomic particles to generate heat.

potassium chloride—a substance derived from potash, used in making fertilizer.

quota—a limit on the quantity of a certain product that can be imported into one country from another.

Symbol of the European Union's currency, the euro, outside the offices of the European Central Bank in Frankfurt, Germany. The European Central Bank controls monetary policies of the European Union. It decides how much currency is issued and sets interest rates.

European Central Bank. The combined EU is a member of the United Nations and World Trade Organization.

One objective of the EU is to ensure that the same policies apply to all members regarding trade and agriculture. Another is to make it easier for citizens to move and trade freely among all the countries.

The European Union has been criticized by some economists both outside and inside its member nations. A notable point of contention is the union's agricultural policy, CAP (Common Agricultural Policy). Among other provisions, it rewards farmers in member countries to promote rural development. Critics have cited the cost of maintaining the CAP policy—billions of dollars annually—and increases in food prices as a result. Some critics note that farmers have been subsidized to produce goods that are not in significant demand. The EU has reformed the CAP policy in recent years.

Free Trade

Free trade is a government's strategy of placing basically no restrictions on exports and imports with certain other nations. For centuries, countries have taken measures to protect their own people and national interests in international trade. For example, they may impose tariffs and/or

Healthy Trade Between the United States and Canada

Canada is the United States' second-leading trade partner, ranked just behind the European Union. By far, the United States is Canada's leading trade partner, with the EU ranked a distant second. Leading imports and exports between the two countries are crude oil and petroleum, motor vehicles and automotive parts, natural gas, *potassium chloride*, aircraft/spacecraft and parts, gold, and wood.

Canada has been a thriving participant in the international trade community. Interestingly, fewer than 1 percent of the world's population live in Canada, but Canada ranks 13th in the world in exports. The country's status as an important world trading partner is expected to continue strengthening.

The United States is the world's largest importer. It ranks third in the world in exports.

quotas on products they import. They apply regulations on the trade of certain goods with certain other countries.

Under a typical free trade pact, the countries agree not to apply regulations, quotas, tariffs, or other taxes and restraints on one another. Economists for a long time have debated the ultimate benefits and disadvantages of those measures on producers and consumers. Most agree that in the long run, free trade can benefit society as a whole.

A free trade agreement that often is in the news is NAFTA (North American Free Trade Agreement). Participating countries are the United States, Canada, and Mexico. NAFTA took effect in 1994. Its purpose was to remove tariffs and trade restrictions among the countries' exports and imports.

Fair Trade

Another strategic issue in the world economy of the twenty-first century is the fair trade movement. Promoters of fair trade policies want to help third world countries succeed and obtain more equitable terms in trading with developed nations. They believe, for example, that producers in poorer countries should be paid comparatively higher prices for the goods they export. Farmers and other workers in dozens of countries work under fair trade policies.

An important technique in fair trade marketing is to arrange for exported products such as coffee to be sold in supermarkets within the purchasing nations. This results in much higher volumes of sales.

The Future of Oil

Humans were aware of surface pools of crude oil thousands of years ago, but they had little use for it. Archaeologists believe some early peoples fueled torches with it and used it to help waterproof boats and clothing. Not until the mid-1800s did a significant demand arise for petroleum. Companies during the Industrial Revolution wanted indoor lighting so they could keep factories operating at night. Residents wanted a cheap fuel for lamps to replace candlelight.

What people for centuries had thought of as "black goo" became "black gold." *Entrepreneurs* began drilling oil wells, first in Germany and then in the United States. For the past 150 years, petroleum has been an extremely important and valuable product in international trade. Today, leading international producers of petroleum and other liquid fuels include the United States, Saudi Arabia, Russia, China, Canada, the United Arab Emirates, Iran, and Iraq.

 Did You Know?

Before crude oil was introduced for lighting household lamps in Europe and America in the 1800s, people used whale oil and tallow candles. Whale oil was expensive. Tallow, derived from animal fat, was smelly.

In 2016, the first new nuclear power plant built in the United States in the 2000s, at Watts Bar in Tennessee. Nuclear power does not produce carbon emissions that contribute to global warming, and so some people prefer it to power generating plants that run on coal or natural gas.

Marchers protest against the Keystone XL Pipeline, which was proposed to transport oil from Canada to refineries in the United States. World leaders are trying to balance the energy needs of the global economy with the fact that burning fossil fuels accelerates the rate of man-made climate change, which could endanger the human race.

The earth's oil reserves are limited. Oil was formed from tiny decomposing organisms over millions of years. Once the existing supply of oil is exhausted, it cannot be replaced. This has led to research into alternate sources of energy. Power sources include coal, wood, natural gas, *nuclear energy*, the sun, and wind.

Still, petroleum products are expected to remain crucial to the world's economy for the foreseeable future. The U.S. Energy Information Administration (EIA) reports that worldwide, an average of 93.7 million barrels of petroleum and other liquid fuels were consumed each day in 2015. The EIA predicts consumption gradually will increase in the next few years.

The Murky Crystal Ball of Global Commerce

Global economists closely watch trade activities among the nations. As in past centuries, trade strategies and techniques will continue to change. Changes will result from the development of new products, shifts in supply and demand, workforce and workplace conditions and characteristics, and world politics.

At the same time, shifts in international commerce will impact the course of national and world politics in the future. That, in turn, will affect supply and demand, labor, and related issues.

 # Text-Dependent Questions

1. What is the standard monetary unit in most nations of the European Union?
2. What three countries participate in NAFTA?

 # Research Project

Conduct a statistical study of the world's leading exporting and importing nations today. Find similar statistics from approximately 20 years ago, and compare. Can you identify developments and trends that have resulted in the shifts in export/import standings?

Organizations to Contact

Canadian Intellectual Property Office
Place du Portage I
50 Victoria Street, Room C-114
Gatineau QC K1A 0C9
Phone: (866) 997-1936
Fax: (819) 953-2476
Website: www.ic.gc.ca/eic/site/cipointer-net-internetopic.nsf/eng/home

Organisation for Economic Co-operation and Development (OECD)
Washington Centre
2001 L Street, NW, Suite 650,
Washington, DC 20036-4922
Phone: (202) 785-6323
Fax: (202) 785-0350
E-mail: washington.contact@oecd.org
Website: www.oecd.org

US Chamber of Commerce
1615 H Street, NW
Washington, DC 20062
Phone: (202) 659-6000
Fax: (202) 463-3126
Email: Americas@uschamber.com
Website: www.uschamber.com

U.S. Copyright Office
101 Independence Ave. S.E.
Washington, D.C. 20559-6000
Phone: (202) 707–3000
Website: http://copyright.gov

U.S. Patent and Trademark Office
USPTO Madison Building
600 Dulany Street
Alexandria, VA 22314
Phone: (800) 786-9199
Fax: (571) 273-0140
Website: www.uspto.gov

World Trade Organization (WTO)
Centre William Rappard
Rue de Lausanne 154
CH-1211 Geneva 21
Switzerland
Phone: +41 (0)22 739-5111
Fax: +41 (0)22 731-4206
Email: enquiries@wto.org
Website: www.wto.org

Series Glossary

barter—the official department that administers and collects the duties levied by a government on imported goods.

bond—a debt investment used by companies and national, state, or local governments to raise money to finance projects and activities. The corporation or government borrows money for a defined period of time at a variable or fixed interest rate.

credit—the ability of a customer to obtain goods or services before payment, based on the trust that payment will be made in the future.

customs—the official department that administers and collects the duties or tariffs levied by a government on imported goods.

debt—money, or something else, that is owed or due in exchange for goods or services.

demurrage—extra charges paid to a ship or aircraft owner when a specified period for loading or unloading freight has been exceeded.

distributor—a wholesaler or middleman engaged in the distribution of a category of goods, esp to retailers in a specific area.

duty—a tax on imported goods.

export—to send goods or services to another country for sale.

Federal Reserve—the central bank of the United States, which controls the amount of money circulating in the US economy and helps to set interest rates for commercial banks.

import—to bring goods or services into a country from abroad for sale.

interest—a fee that is paid in exchange for the use of money that has been borrowed, or for delaying the repayment of a debt.

stock—an ownership interest in a company. Stocks are sold by companies to raise money for their operations. The price of a successful company's stock will typically rise, which means the person who originally bought the stock can sell it and earn a profit.

tariff—a government-imposed tax that must be paid on certain imported or exported goods.

value added tax (VAT)—a type of consumption tax that is placed on a product whenever value is added at each stage of production and at final sale. VAT is often used in the European Union.

World Bank—an international financial organization, connected to the United Nations. It is the largest source of financial aid to developing countries.

Further Reading

Black, Brian C. *Crude Reality: Petroleum in World History*. Lanham, Md.: Rowman & Littlefield Publishers, 2012.

Brown, Stephen R. *Merchant Kings: When Companies Ruled the World, 1600-1900*. New York: St. Martin's Press, 2009.

Helpman, Elhanan. *Understanding Global Trade*. Cambridge, Mass.: Belknap Press, 2011.

McLaren, John. *International Trade*. New York: Wiley Press, 2012.

Richardson, Hazel. *Trade and Commerce in the Ancient World*. New York: Crabtree Publishing Company, 2011.

Internet Resources

www.chamber.ca/advocacy/issues/international-affairs
The International Affairs section of the Canadian
Chamber of Commerce provides information about
international trade and investment developments
that affect Canadian workers.

www.europa.eu
The website for the European Union contains links
to the various administrative and governing bodies
within the organization.

www.naftanow.org
Here, site visitors can learn details about the North
American Free Trade Agreement (NAFTA).

www.cia.gov/library/publications/resources/the-world-factbook
The CIA World Factbook provides a wealth of information about every country in the world, including
a detailed section on each country's economy.

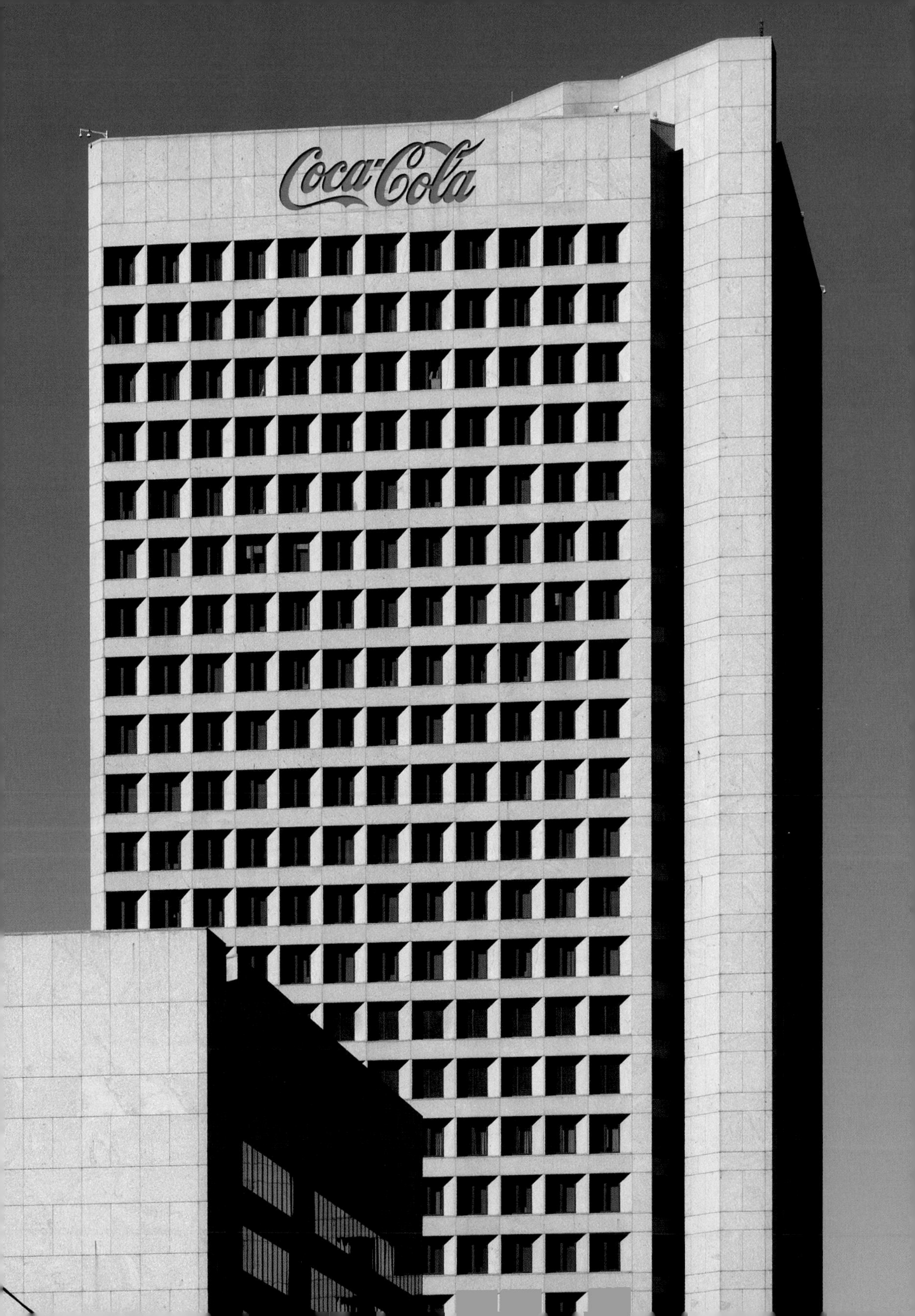
Coca-Cola

Index

Numbers in **bold italic** refer to captions.

About the Author

Daniel E. Harmon is the author of more than 100 books. Much of his research has involved international studies and colonization. He also edits a legal technology newsletter for Thomson Reuters Westlaw, covering such issues as intellectual property. He is a winner of the Excellence in Technology Journalism Award sponsored by The Acer Group and the Computer Museum in Boston. Harmon lives in Spartanburg, South Carolina.